30 Doses

OF MARKETING SUCCESS

A month's worth of tips from a "Marketing Doctor"

JIM KARRH PH.D.

www.themarketingdoctors.net

ISBN: 1-4563-1634-6
ISBN-13:978-1-4563-1634-1

LCCN 2010916284

FOREWORD

This whole thing started in 2000 as an idea for teaching, learning, and creating some customers.

See, at the time my wife and I were moving to a new place (Little Rock, Arkansas) where I had accepted a university teaching job. Because Alison was becoming great with our first child, I had a regular and increasingly prominent reminder that I needed to also pursue incremental business opportunities.

I began doing some homework and soon learned that there was a weekly "must-read" for the state's business community: *Arkansas Business.* After going through a few months of issues, I concluded there was no regular content that would help a business owner, manager, or entrepreneur get a handle on better marketing practices. So, I confidently asked for an appointment with the publication's editorial leadership to talk about a regular column on marketing (which, naturally, would eventually be titled "On Marketing").

Although I had not yet refined the "consultative selling" approach that I use and teach today, the editor (Gwen Moritz, to whom I will always be grateful) somehow allowed me to try a couple of columns.

Those first few columns are not part of this "best of" collection you're currently holding. Still, we had a good initial response from the readers. Businesspeople of nearly all stripes have an interest in marketing, whether they are trying to create a short-term sales blip, find creative inspiration, stay in step with consumer trends, or determine whether their great new idea has any marketplace value.

Over time, my columns would occasionally appear in other publications. With the growth of online media, my stuff was showing up on sites large (Entrepreneur.com) and obscure (don't even get me started). But what I found most rewarding were the e-mails and conversations in which a business leader would say something like, "I made copies of your column on so-and-so and handed them out at the staff meeting."

Since I began the column, my professional path has taken a couple of turns. I willingly left that tenured faculty position—I'm clearly not your typical Ph.D.—in order to join a management group acquiring a 130-year-old consumer brand (in the premium end of the bottled water category) along with its associated distribution and packaging businesses. I embraced the challenge of putting into practice all that lofty teaching and advice I'd been dispensing; within two years, our little company's marketing and public relations program was judged best among members of the International Bottled Water Association. Today I am an independent marketing and sales consultant, professional speaker…and still a columnist. The column has been a constant, and one which I have thoroughly enjoyed.

I hope you enjoy and find value in these writings. I would welcome your comments and ideas; just visit my Web site (www.themarketingdoctors.net) to get in touch.

And, by all means, feel free to share this book at your staff meeting. You might even consider purchasing copies for everyone. Alison and I didn't stop at just one child.

ACKNOWLEDGMENTS

Special thanks are due to:

My wife Alison, for encouraging me while doing most of the really hard work.

My family, for doing all of the loving and supportive things good family members do…and then some.

Gwen Moritz, Jeff Hankins and everyone at Arkansas Business Publishing Group, who gave me my first shot at the exciting world of column-writing a decade ago.

My colleagues at DSG Consulting, Mangan Holcomb Partners, and the VMP Group, for making work fun (generally) and helping me continue to learn.

The many clients, friends, students, and associates who along the way have shaped this book, and my career, in countless and wonderful ways.

CONTENTS

Don't Blame Me

2003

Business hasn't been going the way you had hoped? Well, don't blame me. I tried to tell you—or at least I would have if you'd asked. I left you all sorts of clues, too, but maybe you chose to ignore them.

See, I'm The Consumer, the person you want to be your customer. Whatever your title, whatever your business, you have one job—making me happy. I'm male and female, young and old, simple and complex. I can be loyal and supportive to the point of becoming an evangelist for your business. I'm also quick to anger and easily disappointed, instantly forgetting months or years of satisfying transactions. When I get ticked, I let lots of people know about it. Sometimes I'm fickle, changing my ways for the flimsiest of reasons.

More often, however, I just don't care that much. Don't get me wrong—I care about myself, my family and friends, my appearance, my social position, my budget, and my future. It's just that I don't think much about your business, budget, or goals. In fact, when I feel like you're "selling" me (when the focus is on you and not on me), I tend to shut you off.

Ever go on a date with someone who talked only about himself or herself, showed little interest in you, and failed to pick up your most obvious signals? If so, I'd bet there wasn't a second date. And I think we would know whose tin ear was to blame.

So why am I, The Consumer, reminding you of this now? Well, something's on my mind (and when something becomes top-of-mind, I usually act upon it). Recently, I read where a local business announced its plans to close. In their press release, the owners blamed me for "not supporting their entire facility," or something along those lines. (I usually don't remember the details of news stories or ads, but that doesn't stop me from having my opinions.) In other words, my buying some of their products apparently wasn't enough to satisfy them.

Let's all remember something. It was not and is not my responsibility to support anybody's entire facility—or even part of it. I, The Consumer, care about the products, services, and people I care about. Period. If I'm consistently spending my money to buy 30 percent of your stuff, yet you're mad because I'm not buying the other 70 percent of stuff you're trying to shove down my throat, then one of us needs to reconsider the relationship.

Look, I don't like it when business people have problems; I'm a human being, too. But there are other things that, as The Consumer, I don't like much either: false promises, indifferent service, and poorly made products come to mind.

Before you write me off as a crusty whiner, however, consider how resilient I am. In less than a year and a half, I've digested a horrible terrorist attack on our shores, the threat of foreign war, and the lingering effects of a significant drop in the value of my investments. Have I stopped spending? Have I lost all confidence? Not at all. I'm hanging in there, still consuming away. My consumption comes from the human yearning for the little things that can make life better. I continue to trade the fruits of my labor and savings for your products and services as a tiny expression of trust that tomorrow will come and that I can have some influence over it.

Say what you will about the economy, but look around. The people and businesses who keep their focus on making me happy are still making money, often lots of it. Universities have entire courses devoted to understanding me. Hosts of consultants, research firms, agencies, and others structure their professional lives on figuring me out, and their insights fill libraries, bookstores, and Web sites. You can also watch me, ask me questions, and listen. I may be a little difficult to predict sometimes, but no one needs a Rosetta stone to figure me out. I'm a lot like you.

When you're away from your business, you're The Consumer, too. What's important to you then?

Lessons from the Old Millennium

2002

There are many fresh sources of branding advice available to you these days. I recently found some really old examples that nevertheless might be useful to you.

In "Brand New," Harvard Business School professor Nancy Koehn profiles six entrepreneurs who, in their own ways, paid attention to important social trends and changing preferences; identified some consumer need that didn't exist before; maintained constant two-way communication with customers; insisted on the highest standards of quality; and were relentless, hands-on entrepreneurs, making sure that all areas of their new companies were centered on delivering value to customers. The profiles include business oldies such as H. J. Heinz and Marshall Field along with modern-day brand builders Estee Lauder, Howard Schultz (of Starbucks), and Michael Dell.

Particularly illustrative to me was the story of Josiah Wedgwood, who founded his own pottery workshop in 1759 and eventually created a company and brand that have thrived for almost 250 years.

At the time, most Britons ate from wood or pewter plates. Wedgwood recognized that times were changing and that middle-class British consumers increasingly were able to buy household goods that others could scarcely imagine. He also saw that consumers wanted novel goods that at some level could connect them to the magnificent homes, furnishings, and gardens of the rich. In response, Wedgwood developed an improved creamware, an attractive white pottery that closely resembled more expensive porcelain.

I doubt that Wedgwood ever thought of his operation as a brand; for him, it was simply a business. But long before the lingo and tools of modern-day branding emerged, Wedgwood understood—and, more importantly, diligently applied—these wonderful brand-building principles:

* Gaining publicity and prestige. Wedgwood and his partner, Thomas Bentley, worked hard and accepted low profits on aristocratic and royal commissions. After gaining an aristocratic sale, Wedgwood advertised it to the larger, more profitable market. It was a deft use of celebrity endorsement.

* Linking his promises to the customer's experience. Most merchants of the day tended to store goods in back rooms, only bringing them out for interested shoppers. Wedgwood's London showrooms were full of retailing innovations, such as the use of display cabinets and wide aisles that allowed customers to move about easily. Drawing upon the consumer's desire for novelty, Wedgwood insisted that displays of table and dessert services be changed every few days to encourage frequent repeat visits.

* Smart expansion into new markets. Wedgwood followed his sound domestic marketing strategy while moving into international markets. He began by focusing on British ambassadors and their wives, who were likely to be moved from one

European capital to another (taking with them their preference for Wedgwood goods). He also courted aristocrats and nobles in France, Germany, Turkey, and even China. By 1783, Wedgwood was exporting almost 80 percent of his production.

* Establishing and leveraging a brand. At the time, very few luxury goods were known by their manufacturers' names (Chippendale furniture and Meissen porcelain were among the exceptions). Most potters did not mark their products in any way; those who did tended to use either a symbol or the location of the factory as an identifying mark. Wedgwood changed this practice by impressing his name on the unfired clay, which both made his pieces less vulnerable to forgery and turned each of his creations into an advertisement for the Wedgwood name. Wedgwood then used the power of his brand name to charge a premium, keeping his prices well above industry averages. "Low prices," he wrote in 1772, "must beget a low quality in the manufacture, which will beget contempt, which will beget neglect, and disuse, and there is the end of the trade."

* Customer satisfaction programs. In exchange for the higher prices they paid, Wedgwood's customers received unprecedented support. Customers received free shipping anywhere in England, compensation for any damage to goods in transport, and the first recorded example of a "satisfaction or your money back" guarantee.

As Professor Koehn wrote, "Wedgwood and Bentley understood that in the emerging consumer society, marketing was as important as manufacturing." And this came during the time that those on our side of the Atlantic were colonists.

When Experts Go Wrong

2003

It's easy to have a snicker at the expense of so-called experts. Some forecasts we heard and read concerning a war in Iraq were so outrageously wrong that you have to wonder who hands out "expert" labels. On the other hand, some experts come up with explanations that are so safe (and thus banal) as to be useless. The complexity of business means that most of us need expert help on a regular basis. Perhaps your business hires or will hire consultants to either provide ongoing direction or help you solve a specific problem. To some extent, most of us incorporate experts' views into our evaluations of the economy, legislative moves, consumer trends, and the like. So, with true expertise a valuable commodity in business, whom can you trust? In this column, I'll share the results of research into business expertise—which should help you know when to pay attention to what the experts say.

* Expertise is not equivalent to experience. These areas are related, but only in one direction: Experts almost always have experience in a particular area, but not everyone with experience is an expert. (Don't we all know people who have been doing the same wrong thing for a long time?) In studies of forecasting accuracy across many industries, lots of experienced professionals get their clocks cleaned by less-experienced

colleagues. True expertise combines some level of experience with specific knowledge.

* Expertise is deep rather than wide. Experts tend to be broadly intelligent people, but true expertise is typically confined to one rather narrow area. While oncologists and cardiologists, for example, received similar training in anatomy, genetics, and biochemistry, you wouldn't seek out the former to treat a heart problem. *Arkansas Business* named me the Top Prognosticator of 2002 for anticipating problems at McDonald's—but that was a relatively easy call for a marketing expert. Some experts (particularly those with some measure of fame and media access) tend to go public with pronouncements and predictions outside of their realm of knowledge—and embarrass themselves in the process. In a business setting, you hope to deal with outside experts who both know their specialty and have at least enough appreciation of its relationships to other areas to make practical recommendations. But that's something you'll need to consider carefully, because there's nothing about being an expert in one area that necessarily makes you an expert in any other area.

* Experts approach problems differently than do novices. Controlled studies of equity analysts (those who had a history of high accuracy in predicting company earnings versus those proven to be less accurate) found that experts quickly sift through data in an order they choose (rather than in the order it is listed). In other words, the experts keep in their heads a model of the most important factors to consider. They actively seek information on those factors and know to ignore irrelevant data. The result? Experts are not only more accurate than novices, they also arrive at decisions faster.

* Expertise helps with certain kinds of decisions—but not all. If the situation is very simple, then you don't need to pay an expert to tell you what to do. If it's complex but involves some really new pattern of relationships (meaning an expert can't apply what he or she has learned), then an expert probably can't offer more insight than could a novice. This might explain why experts don't have great track records in predicting abrupt changes, such as the impact of innovative products and technologies. However, there is a large category of problems and opportunities where experts thrive. Complex issues that conform to familiar patterns lend themselves to experts' finely tuned diagnoses. For example, if you're considering a brand extension (introducing a new product under an existing brand name), some marketing experts could hone in on success factors pretty quickly because there are several decades of brand-extension history and research available.

In sum, research suggests that experts can help you bore through the complexity of some issues in ways that will efficiently help your business. You just need to be a smart shopper. But you didn't need an expert to tell you that.

Is Marketing Art or Science?

2003

Do you ever hear (or even say) things like this around your organization: "I know this business, and no outside person or computer can tell me anything I don't already know?" Or, perhaps you're more likely to hear, "None of us is any smarter than these computers, and we have to go by the numbers."

These very different perspectives cut to the heart of an ongoing art-versus-science debate about marketing management. I recently discovered a study that put the debate to the test, in the form of "database model versus manager intuition." The results are an eye-opener for any decision maker who needs to make accurate forecasts and sound choices.

The study is neither new nor particularly well known (at least outside the academic realm); it was published in 1990 in the journal *Management Science* by researchers Robert Blattberg and Stephen Hoch.

But before examining the particulars of the study, let's review why intelligent people could find themselves on either side of the debate.

There are good reasons to believe that managers' experience and intuition should drive decision making. Despite the strides made in artificial intelligence systems, computer scientists are still a long way from developing systems that actually mimic human problem solving. No mathematical model does very well at predicting change; models are consistent yet rigid. No mathematical model can come up with a breakthrough idea or innovative approach. Expert human beings are able to incorporate a wide range of qualitative, "soft" pieces of information—while computer models can only incorporate variables that are quantified or categorized.

On the other hand, there are many good reasons to believe that managers should set aside their gut intuition and instead rely on objective, quantitative data for better decisions. We know, for example, that human beings carry a host of biases into their decisions. We tend to be overconfident. We choose information selectively, in ways that tend to match our prior expectations. We can become tired, bored, and emotional. We often make decisions for personal or political reasons.

So, which is it? Are most decisions best left to managers' intuition, or should forecasting models drive decisions?

In their study, Blattberg and Hoch examined two categories of forecasting situations: retail buyers' predictions of catalog sales of specific fashion merchandise, and brand managers' predictions of coupon redemption rates. In all, they examined five separate forecasting tasks using real-time marketplace data. Experienced managers were recruited for the relevant tasks and asked to give their forecasts; the managers' forecasts were then compared to the purely data-driven predictions of computer models.

In most cases, managers were nearly as accurate in their predictions as were the computer models. The real payoff, however, came in considering the two together. Combining the predictions of managers and databases produced forecasts up to 16 percent more accurate than either alone.

Blattberg and Hoch wrote, "Model and manager forecasts are complementary sources of information that increase in predictive accuracy when considered in tandem." In plain language, they're simply confirming that database models and managers' gut reactions have strengths which overlap yet still differ markedly.

Even more interesting was the mix of model and manager that was most accurate in predicting marketplace success: 50-50. The authors tested many different combinations of weighting schemes, but an equal mix of art (intuition) and science (data) proved best.

The authors' conclusions included this: "Both statistical and human inputs should guide final decisions." I agree. There's no reason to think computer models could or should replace the well-honed intuition of experienced managers.

However, really smart managers also recognize the value of adding objective data (past results, market research, and the like) to whatever their guts tell them.

The Shortcuts Consumers Take

2003

How do consumers make choices? Most of the marketing guides and textbooks I see include intricate flow charts that represent the process of consumer decision making. The assumption is that human beings, in their role as consumers, are rational, multistage problem solvers.

Don't believe it.

I'm not saying consumers never engage in reasoned decision making. It's just that, when it comes to making decisions, we all have limits on our time, ability, and interest. Further, whether we're acting as consumers, managers, or investors, we tend to distort information and take a lot of mental shortcuts in order to get to our decisions.

In this column, I'll share four common consumer shortcuts (what we consumer-psychologist types call "heuristics"). By recognizing these typical thinking patterns, you'll not only be a more effective marketer, but you'll also be a better consumer.

* The Availability Bias. We all tend to evaluate problems and issues based upon the most recent "similar" case that comes to mind. That might be due to personal experiences; there's a direct connection between the number of people you know

who smoke and the total percentage of Americans you think smoke. Similarly, vivid events from our lives or the media tend to stay top-of-mind. For example, if you see a lot of media coverage of former Enron or WorldCom executives being herded into court, then you're likely to guess that executives commit fraud more frequently than they actually do.

Another powerful form of this bias is the "recency effect," our tendency to remember the things at the end of a list. It's no accident that the IRS tends to publicize arrests for tax evasion in February and March, so as to be top of-mind for April filers. The implications for marketing: You need to stay top-of-mind with consumers, even if you're well-known. And if you want something to stand out in a consumer's mind, don't let it get lost in the middle of your messages to them.

* The Confirmation Bias. When we make a decision, we actively look for things that will confirm our decision as a good one and avoid anything that would point out problems. When presented with evidence that an opinion or decision is wrong, we tend to disregard or dispute that evidence. For example, most of us skip over articles or editorials in a newspaper that seem to conflict with our beliefs. The implication for marketing: once you've brought in new customers, help them feel good by giving them evidence they made a wise choice by buying from you.

* The Representativeness Heuristic. This heuristic relates to the ways we judge some event or object to be part of a category—and it rears its head in several ways. For example, we tend to ignore sample sizes when judging the likelihood of events. A consumer might know that Yugos have a terrible service record overall but choose to buy one anyway because they

knew someone who had a Yugo and "didn't have any trouble with it." We also tend to underestimate the effect of pure chance. Results from lottery entries show that when a series of numbers is announced as a "winner," more players will select those same numbers during the next several drawings. The implication for marketing: anecdotes and stories tend to short-circuit consumers' views of what is typical.

* Anchoring and Adjustment. "Anchoring" refers to the starting point for making a judgment—and most of us don't make enough of an adjustment from an anchor even if it isn't particularly credible. For example, if I asked a group of people whether the population of Arkansas was greater or less than five million, then later asked them what they thought the population is, most of the answers would cluster around five million (at least for those people who weren't sure of the correct answer). Similarly, when one party to a negotiation suggests a price or condition, the other party is likely to base its counteroffer on that particular anchor. The implication for marketing: if you're in a negotiation and the other person makes the first bid, don't assume that this is actually close to his or her final price.

Do You Communicate Well?

2003

It appears that most managers are kidding themselves—and missing valuable opportunities in the process.

According to a 2002 survey, conducted nationwide with a sample of more than 1,100 employees and reported in the *Harvard Management Communication Letter*, 86 percent of respondents said their bosses believed themselves to be effective communicators. However, only 17 percent of those employees believed their bosses to be good communicators in practice. Those results would imply that about two-thirds of American managers are delusional (at least when it comes to their communication skills).

I'm preparing this column while in New Orleans at a marketers' conference, where most of the speakers and presenters could use a little help in the communication department, too.

How about you? Are you a good communicator, both inside and outside of your organization? I believe almost any boss can be more effective in communication without drastically altering his or her personal style, simply by following a few guidelines.

First, think strategically about what it is you hope to accomplish. What do you want the other person(s) to think, feel, and do? I've seen many cases in which a boss or manager lost track of the overall goal; the manager was, for example, blunt when employees needed to feel understood or too big-picture when employees simply needed to know which steps to take next.

Second, understand that you will be sending messages in a variety of ways (even without planning to do so). According to Boyd Clarke and Ron Crossland, authors of *The Leader's Voice*, there are three essential elements to communication effectiveness: facts, emotions, and symbols. The authors claim that in order to "move people to action, help them understand and deepen their appreciation, and gain more insight and passion about their work, you need to have all three."

Here are some ideas for bringing those three elements to life in your personal communication efforts:

* Tell a story, but make it count. Effective storytelling doesn't mean starting each speech or conversation with "So this guy goes into a bar…" There's a fine line between jabbering about your own experiences (just because there's a momentarily captive audience) and using those experiences and emotions in order to connect with others. It can seem dangerous for leaders to share their fears and dreams in a business setting. But by effectively incorporating personal stories into their communication style, leaders tell others what they feel and— importantly—why. That humanizes the leader in a positive way and tends to rally others in support.

* Offer facts and data—in measured doses, and always with interpretation. By themselves, numbers aren't that enlightening; it helps to offer relative, relevant context, such as historical results, competitors' results, industry averages, regional or

national comparisons, and the like. If you only tell your staff, "We're going to grow sales revenue by 8 percent in 2004," you'll probably meet a lot of resistance (spoken or unspoken). However, if you say, "The forecast for our industry overall next year is 6 percent sales growth, and because of *x*, *y*, and *z*, we can make 8 percent," it's more likely the goal will be embraced.

* Use symbols to reinforce your message. Symbols can be quite powerful, and they can take many forms. Logos, quotes, metaphors, rituals, and ceremonies all carry symbolic meaning. Clarke and Crossland offer the example of management's efforts to refocus the brand positioning of Turner Network Television in 2001. For years, TNT had aired a highly varied mix of programs. With greater competition from better-targeted cable networks, TNT was in danger of losing its identity—and, ultimately, viewers. TNT hired Steve Koonin, a former Coca-Cola marketing executive, as its general manager. Koonin wanted to position TNT as the channel for drama (you've probably seen the "We Know Drama" tag line). Management helped reinforce this new positioning among employees with an internal program called the "Drammy Awards." Among the recipients of a Drammy (for Most Dramatic Meeting) was a pregnant vice president whose water broke during a staff meeting. You can be sure that story was shared informally among all TNT employees, probably with some comment such as, "Yep, we really do know drama."

So Say Something

2004

"The boss said to change the sign, so I did."

I saw this a couple of months ago on the marquee outside of a Little Rock retailer. I've also seen similar versions through the years in Atlanta, Tuscaloosa, Charleston, and even Statesboro, Georgia. It was clever the first time.

The sign reminded me of how popular those portable marquees became a couple of decades ago (the ones on wheels, typically with a flashing arrow on top). In my hometown, they popped up like mushrooms after a rainy weekend. For a while, the merchants who bought or rented these things made a real effort to change the messages and stay relevant to the consumers driving by. Before long, however, most of those merchants had pretty much stopped trying—and just left the same message up for months at a time. There's nothing like a few sagging, mismatched, sun-bleached letters spelling "Sale" in the middle of a big sign to keep consumers excited, huh?

Things seem a bit better today. Many retailers have incorporated marquees into their signs which may be changed as needed. During a recent afternoon spent driving along a couple of Little Rock thoroughfares, I kept track of the content in the marquees I saw. Here is my rough count:

* About twenty businesses used their signs to announce sales. Not a bad move, actually.

* Four businesses had a message about a new product. Ditto.

* Two marquees simply repeated the name of the business (both were located directly under signs that featured the name of the business). Not incrementally helpful.

* In an indication that labor markets are stronger, two businesses used a marquee in order to announce "Help Wanted."

* Three businesses used the marquee to offer a non-sales message (a tribute to the late President Reagan, a "when in doubt, pray," and a "life is like laundry..." bit of philosophy at a laundromat).

* One marquee had only the ever-uplifting "Closed."

* Four businesses had absolutely nothing on their marquees, each of which is passed by thousands of vehicles every day.

Many of us have valuable platforms through which we can speak to customers and prospects—so we ought to use them. Four businesses failing to say anything at all on their marquee seems like four too many to me.

In your business, such recurring platforms might include signs, your storefront, a Web site, a newsletter, the bills you send to customers or even your involvement in supporting community events and nonprofits. Are you getting the results you should from these regular communication opportunities? I suggest you occasionally assess your efforts, starting with these questions:

* Who's in charge? I would make sure it's someone who understands the marketing strategy of the business, knows the importance of the messages sent to the marketplace—and can spell. Otherwise, well…the boss did just say to "change the sign"…

* Are you serving fresh content or leftovers? As consumers, all of us develop some pretty powerful filters for our daily encounters with the world. We tend to tune out the familiar, only noticing the novel, negative, and vivid. So, a marquee or Web site that never varies will quickly lose its effectiveness. Keep the content fresh enough to gain attention.

* Are you consistent? Although the form of your messages will need periodic changes (see above), the underlying message should have some consistency over time. For example, if your marketing strategy is based upon high product quality and customer service, then don't allow your messages to jump around to sales and price considerations.

* Are you relevant? Sales, new products, and simple, uplifting messages can all strike a chord with at least some prospective customers. One area veterinary clinic regularly combines publicity for a pet adoption service with good community relations by posting messages on its marquee such as, "Come meet Opal, our gem of a cat." Hokey, perhaps, but certainly memorable and probably effective.

And to those four businesses with nothing to say: How about "Sale"?

Pricing Myths and Musts

2005

Whether you're dealing in products or services, and whether you're big or small, your business needs to make good decisions about prices. However, among the major areas of marketing, pricing is the least researched and least understood. There are a lot of misconceptions out there that could cost you business.

In this column, I'll outline a few of the lingering myths about pricing. In an upcoming column, I will share examples of how technology and information flow are forever changing the way companies are negotiating prices with consumers.

* Myth 1: Most companies are sophisticated in researching and setting prices.

According to the American Marketing Association, more than 80 percent of companies responding to a 2001 survey reported doing little or no serious pricing research. That result mirrors the data from McKinsey & Company's Pricing Benchmark Survey.

* Myth 2: Pricing should be based upon cost.

What consumers are willing to pay has nothing to do with your costs—which are unknown and irrelevant to consumers—and everything to do with alternatives, quality perceptions, emotion, and perceptions of fairness. Yes, you need to have a clear view of cost so that you understand the profit implications of pricing decisions—but not for the express purpose of setting price.

* Myth 3: If one or more competitors are cutting prices, you have to do the same or perish.

Kent Monroe, professor of marketing at the University of Illinois at Urbana-Champaign, has studied pricing decisions more than any other person I know. He frequently uses the following real-world story to illustrate how consumers tend to confound conventional wisdom about prices. A packaged-goods manufacturer had developed and marketed two versions of a product, A and B. The versions were nearly identical except that version B's label and packaging gave it a higher-quality look. The company priced version A at $14.95 and version B at $18.95. As you might expect, version A was the better-selling product, albeit at much lower margins. After a while, a competitor came in with a premium version that was priced much higher at $34.95. So guess what happened to the original company's products? Within a short time, version B became the best seller. As Monroe says, theory tells us this can't happen—but it does. There's a natural tendency to match competitors, but if you're doing a great job with your marketing, consumers won't find competitors' offerings as easy substitutes for your offering.

* Myth 4: Consumers are efficient in making price comparisons.

The truth is closer to the feeling you get when a spouse or friend says, "Do you notice anything different about me today?" Consumers' comparisons are typically skewed in several ways. First, most consumers are swayed by reference prices, their mental starting points. Reference prices may come from a consumer's experience, advertising she remembers, or the advice of a friend. Prices that stray from a reference price stick out, and usually not for the better. Second, consumers pay more attention to relative prices than to absolute prices. A price rise from $1.00 to $1.25 is perceived more strongly than a rise from $1.50 to $1.75, for example. Finally, as you might expect, research into price elasticities shows that consumers are more sensitive to perceived price hikes than to perceived price cuts. The implication is that it's easier to lose current customers by jacking prices too high than it is to gain new customers by lowering prices.

* Myth 5: Consumers perceive one "good" price for any particular product or service.

There is no one sweet spot to hit on pricing; consumers almost always have a range of acceptable prices for any given potential purchase. The upper limit adjusts according to factors like the number of perceived alternatives and the current level of satisfaction and loyalty. The lower limit shifts according to quality perceptions. Yes, there is a point where prices can seem too low to the consumer—particularly when quality is important (think of someone offering to prepare your tax returns at the last minute for $9.99).

Marketing and Change

2005

The recent Arkansas Executive Summit was planned around a compelling issue for business leaders: change. Several speakers and expert panelists addressed the topic of environmental and organizational change from their experiences across industries.

For this third annual event, I had the opportunity to spend the morning in the audience rather than on the panel (probably a big improvement over the previous two summits). As I was making notes and attempting to synthesize the most compelling points made by the speakers, I kept returning to five "Cs" that I wanted to take back and share within my organization: consciousness, comfort, culture, consistency, and customer.

"Consciousness" describes an active state of looking for areas where change is needed—a state the most successful companies are embracing. These executives aren't just gritting their teeth and changing what is absolutely necessary. Instead, they make it a point to constantly scan the environment—as well as their companies' capabilities and opportunities—and embrace change as a competitive advantage.

"Comfort" is not a psychological state usually associated with constant change. This is something successful business leaders readily admit. We're all uncomfortable with change. So, these executives take that factor into account and recognize the need for consistently "selling" the need for change within their companies.

"Culture" is a fuzzy yet particularly important factor. Nearly every speaker pointed to the CEO as the person who must take a visible, positive role as primary change agent within the organization. As Russ Harrington said, "Who is the champion in your company?" If you don't know, then your company has problems. Further, the speakers emphasized that employees must feel the freedom to experiment and fail without getting hammered from the top. This factor also encompasses another C—communication—which is important for both understanding cultural barriers to change and conveying the direction of the company.

"Consistency" in this context is not to be confused with stagnation or an overreliance on tradition. Rather, it is the importance of a common purpose and set of values within the organization. Some speakers talked of the importance of consistency within the management team when the outside world is changing so quickly. In short, successful companies in rapidly changing environments need a steady rudder.

The final theme I inferred—"customer"—raised some very interesting questions about market research, intuition, and the cost of market leadership. As I've noted in previous columns, the conventional wisdom of a "first-mover advantage" is a myth in most industries; being first to market is no guarantee of long-term market success. Does this mean that speed is overrated?

At the same time, using surveys or other research tools to lead new-product development can be a losing proposition. Chief Executive Officer Charles Morgan noted that Acxiom's new-product successes have come despite the fact that the company didn't ask customers what they thought they needed before moving ahead. But doesn't successful change come from an uncompromising focus on customers' evolving needs and alternatives?

My advice is to consider your industry and the rate of technological change. If technologies and alternatives tend to stay fairly constant in your line of business, then today's consumer perceptions can indeed help you predict tomorrow's market results. On the other hand, people have a difficult time imagining a product, service, or technology that doesn't yet exist—and the hypothetical purchasing behavior expressed in surveys regarding such technologies rarely bears any resemblance to the real world.

That doesn't mean you shouldn't conduct research or otherwise pay attention to customers and other consumers as part of your change strategy. To the contrary: while most consumers aren't accurate in predicting their future behavior, they're pretty good about conveying their current likes, dislikes, opinions, and frustrations. Let those insights into your customers' guts drive your own gut about the areas of change needed in your company.

Theory Meets Reality

2005

It has been just over a year now since I left a tenured academic position in the University of Arkansas at Little Rock's College of Business to take on a marketing position back in the private sector. A friend who's still in the ivory tower (in another state) recently asked me how things were going, in an interesting way: "So what have you been learning?"

Academics can be funny in the way they ask questions.

That question was far different than the one I usually get from friends and acquaintances who aren't academics: "So what's it like being in the real world?" My reply is that I've never been away from it, because (1) I once owned an unfortunately small business and (2) even while an academic, I consulted and otherwise took part in real-world activities.

Having had feet in both realms, I have learned that the business world and the ivory tower, very broadly speaking, can learn a few things from each other.

* The value of theory. Some in the private sector speak derisively about theories, as if theories are always so far removed from reality as to be nothing more than intellectual exercises. However, in general, I find that business decision makers

can profit from thinking a little more theoretically. It's been said that "nothing is as practical as a good theory," and if you consider what a theory really is, you might agree. A theory is essentially a consistent and comprehensive way of explaining how some part of the world works. If you consider all the possible factors that might impact the success of even a smaller, well-bounded project—such as designing a direct-mail campaign—then you'll appreciate the necessity of being able to focus on a few critical success factors. A predictive model of, say, which printed images and words are most likely to be noticed and lead to action (which is a theory) is vital to getting the campaign somewhere close to right the first time.

* The need for speed. As a graduate student, I was once told by a faculty mentor to revise a research paper as quickly as I could do a thorough job. I asked him whether a week's time was too long; he smiled and said, "Academics have a different concept of turnaround time than you do, Jim." (He was thinking about a two-month time frame.) Because of both the nature of the questions they address and the lack of administrative support, professors tend to take their time. In business, of course, that is sometimes a formula for failure and missed opportunity.

* Giving credit where it's due. The culture of academic research demands that one learn from prior studies, explain how one's work expands current knowledge, and advise other researchers of opportunities for them to further extend your work in the future. This approach, while time consuming and occasionally tiresome for the researcher, has the benefit of looking at knowledge as a continuously improving process. It also implicitly recognizes that there aren't very many truly original ideas floating around out there. Business people can adopt

the best parts of this approach by actively looking for data and case studies from the past—and not pretending that insight and ideas just come out of thin air.

* The necessity of being a team player. Academics can be successful by following a fairly lonely professional path. Professors choose the research path that interests them as well as the outlets where they'd prefer to publish and promote that research. Professors also are given wide latitude in the ways they teach their courses (and team teaching is very rare). In short, academics are largely in control of the planning and execution of their career plans. Business executives, on the other hand, depend on others to carry out their visions and strategies. Much of any CEO's time and energy is devoted to the art of recruiting, evaluating, motivating, and rewarding other people.

I think that business leaders, by both their nature and experience, tend to be better as team members.

There is one other similarity I've found between professors and business leaders. In both cases, other people (their students or employees) have to sometimes pretend to be interested in what they say.

Inside Marketers' Minds

2005

An interesting collection of short marketing essays, part of Aspatore Books' *Inside the Minds* series for current and aspiring business executives and law firm partners, has just been published. The book, *Succeeding as a Marketing Executive*, has eleven chapters on various marketing leadership topics, each written by a different currently active chief marketing officer or similarly titled executive.

Before I summarize for you some of these senior marketers' insights, full disclosure is in order: I am one of the chapter contributors. Still, don't take this as a self-serving book plug; I receive zippo—other than one free copy of the book—from the publisher.

(Well, at least I know that *I* am not compensated in any way. If I find out the other contributors are, then I'll be peeved. Maybe I should have negotiated harder, huh?)

The other contributors represent top practitioners across a range of industries, including investment services (Anne Nelson of Ameritrade), retailing (Edward Carroll Jr. of Carson Pirie Scott & Company), business services (Andrew Ceccon of OnlineBenefits Incorporated), consumer packaged goods (Jordi Ferre of

Wise Foods), software products (Susan Huberman of Iomega), and Internet services (Gina Lombardi of Qualcomm).

Here are some of the bits of wisdom I found in my cohorts' writings:

* An effective marketing leader has to "get it" from both inside and outside the organization. As Nelson writes, "The head of marketing, more than any other person in a company, needs to be the keeper of the brand and a consistent advocate for the end customer."

* Creativity, in its many forms, matters. As Ceccon observes, "People often mistake creativity as an innate talent only for writers and artists. Not true. It means breaking down barriers and trying to look at a problem from new angles. It requires an open mind and the willingness to bring your whole self to work, not just the part of you that wears the business clothes."

* On the other hand, creative skills alone are not sufficient for long-term success; you also need to understand the numbers and how to drive measurable results. Carroll writes, "In general, marketing departments must focus on fact-based analysis rather than relying solely on intuition or subjective factors. Success is in the details of the businesses, and it is important for a marketing executive to begin applying more science than art in determining strategies that will differentiate them from the competition and be cost effective as well."

* Marketing requires both resolute devotion to strategy and a certain flexibility as to methods. Huberman writes, "I would say that being a marketing executive is analogous to being silk. Silk is a smooth, fluid fabric, yet it's extremely strong

and durable....You need to maintain fluidity in order to take advantage of new opportunities, but you also need to be very strong in delivering your message and staying true to your brand."

* Even great messages, by themselves, won't guarantee marketplace success. Carroll: "In retail, 'nothing happens until the last ten feet.' That's when the customer makes a decision, interacts with the store associate, and either makes a purchase or does not. The greatest advertising in the world is not meaningful unless all the other parts work."

* If other people in your organization don't understand marketing's contribution—a likely scenario—then it's up to you to educate and energize them. As Huberman writes, "Many people view marketing as discretionary spending or a luxury item rather than as an essential investment. The misconception exists because for years there was no visibility in the role of marketing and little emphasis on marketing measurement and return on investment. I have found that with assuming more accountability and providing more transparency in terms of what works and what doesn't, we can build internal support for the marketing function as a value driver."

Huberman also had my favorite single line in the book: "Early in my career, I had a boss tell me that marketing is like sex, because everyone thinks they're good at it."

Why Sponsors Sponsor

2005

It's hunting season again—and that doesn't just involve things with feathers and fur.

Most of us on the corporate side of the ledger have gone through budgeting processes that include plans for partnerships, event support and sponsorships, and other philanthropic activities. On the other side, leaders of not-for-profits have been planning ways of securing corporate partnerships in an increasingly competitive fundraising environment.

In this column, I'd like to share one marketer's ideas and biases as well as the conclusions of an interesting article on corporate philanthropy. Taken together, they might make things easier for both the hunter and hunted.

A strong shift in corporate giving has become apparent in recent years: More companies are demanding a link between philanthropy and bottom-line business objectives. One example of a big corporation taking a hard, strategic look at its giving is highlighted in Keith Epstein's article "Philanthropy, Inc.," published in the summer 2005 issue of the *Stanford Social Innovation Review* (I'll take a wild guess that you haven't yet thumbed through that particular issue). Raytheon, the nation's fifth-largest defense contractor, is carrying out a far more focused approach to philanthropy than was the case when the company's executives acted to change its giving practices seven years ago. Around its Tucson, Arizona, missile factory, Raytheon decided to focus on math and science education; the primary objective was to fill its workforce pipeline. "We have engineers and scientists, and we need engineers and scientists," said a Raytheon manager. "Why would we fund a program for nurses' aides?"

One not-for-profit fundraiser quoted in the article believes that most companies have four criteria for entering into or contributing to partnerships: (1) the cause must be relevant to the company's products or services; (2) there must be a good fit with the overall company brand; (3) the partnership must align with a company mission; and (4) the company must believe it can achieve some measurable business result through the partnership.

Yes, things have changed from the days of just being a "good corporate citizen."

So what should you do if you're the person trying to gain corporate support for your cause or organization? I don't think you need to dilute your own mission or otherwise fully submit to corporate profit interests. It would help you, however, to simply see any proposed partnership or support from your prospect's perspective—in short, to approach the process as any good marketer would. What's in it for him, aside from just the glow he'll get from being associated with you?

Here is my company's perspective. We publish a sponsorship guide on our Web site that encourages any group asking for our help to consider the following:

35

* Lead time. Would we have enough time to gain the full benefit of our support, or is this a last-minute request?

* Is someone in charge? Unfortunately, many events are run by a committee or other rather loosely connected group; that spells trouble for sponsors, who typically want to deal with one person who has knowledge and authority.

* A clear sense of what you want. Are you looking for cash, product, executives' time, or some combination? Have you considered all the costs associated with your request?

* A clear sense of what you're willing to provide. Do you have a membership list that would be useful to sponsors? What are the limitations you would place on sponsors when it comes to leveraging your event and membership? (By the way, I absolutely think it's a good idea to have some limitations and enforce them. You have to keep the integrity of your own brand.)

* Publicity and communications. How will the event or cause be promoted? Do you have media partners who will help you get the word out? Is there a really good spokesperson and communications structure?

* Why us and not someone else? Everyone wants to feel special. Before approaching potential partners or sponsors, I would review publicly available information (products, profiles, mission statements, etc.) to get a sense of "fit." I'll resist the urge to share specifics, but I can tell you that we have been approached by folks seeking product and/or cash who were obviously not in concert with our image or markets.

Happy hunting.

Does Cindy Crawford Work?

2006

There she was, in all of her exquisiteness, even including that signature mole.

Cindy Crawford, one of the original supermodels, was gracing the page of a business/lifestyle magazine in an ad for Omega watches. Under the headline "Cindy Crawford's choice," she of hundreds of runways, covers, and videos was photographed simply in black and white displaying Omega-on-wrist.

I thought: maybe not a great implementation of celebrity endorsement.

You might reasonably inquire, "Jim, how could you possibly look at a photo of Cindy Crawford and think about marketing strategy?" Answer: This is what I do. It's my cross to bear.

Companies have used endorsers for decades, of course. In fact, the category of watches produced one of America's first uses of celebrity endorsement in advertising. Way back in 1870, the noted orator and minister Henry Ward Beecher appeared in a *Harper's Weekly* ad touting Waltham watches. Today, it's estimated that one in five network TV ads uses some form of celebrity endorsement.

In general, the marketing communication format for endorsements tends to fall into one of three categories:

* "You don't know me, but you know my friend." If your brand is new, unknown, and/or mundane, then hitching it to a well-known person's star power may provide a mechanism to get the brand on consumers' radar screens. The downside is that those consumers tend to pay much more attention to your friend than to you.

* "You really like me." Likeability is a huge issue in advertising. On the national celebrity front, Marketing Evaluations Incorporated has been developing and offering "Q Score" results for four decades; the Q Score is a measurement of likeability. Another way of presenting likeable endorsers is to find individuals to whom customers feel they can relate—either actual customers in testimonials or next-door types with a general, everyday appeal.

* "I know what I'm talking about." On occasion, the endorser is valuable because of his or her specific expertise. It is no coincidence that so many ads for over-the-counter medications, diet plans, and the like have endorsers with lab coats. The thread of expertise may be quite thin, yet it's still effective. The late actor Ricardo Montalban, assumed to have an appreciation for luxury around the world, famously sold Chrysler cars with "fine Corinthian leather." (Remember, too, the line "I'm not a doctor, but I play one on TV," spoken by a soap-opera actor in ads for Vicks Formula 44 cough syrup during the 1980s.)

Regardless of the marketing tactic used, for endorser effectiveness the ultimate criteria are attractiveness and trustworthiness. Those attributes assume different levels of importance to the consumer depending upon the type of purchase that is represented.

Low-cost, low-risk, familiar products and services are driven by the attractiveness criterion. The person deciding on, say, which chip to buy doesn't feel the need for consulting a chip expert (assuming such an expert even exists). Seeing Jay Leno crunch Doritos may be all that is needed to guide that type of purchase.

For higher-cost, higher-risk purchases, the attractiveness of an endorser is far less relevant than is trustworthiness. Financial planners, physicians, real estate professionals, and the manufacturers of expensive goods need—if they choose to use endorsers—representatives who are perceived to have both objectivity and expertise.

Michael Jordan has been a great endorser for a number of different types of products because he brings a rare combination of likeability and expertise. (I still don't understand the Ball Park Franks deal, however. Are we to believe hot dogs were part of his training regimen?) Most endorsers can only get away with staking out one criterion or the other.

Given all this, you might finally inquire, "So wouldn't you want Cindy Crawford to be an endorser for your company if you could afford her?" Answer: Given Crawford's assumed expertise in beauty, health, and vitality…well, you bet your last lip mole I would.

The Sound of Carelessness

2006

One of the great challenges in marketing is to come up with appropriate names for products, services, and companies. These days, with tens of thousands of names already out there, it seems the best and most obvious stuff has been taken.

By the way, if the whole exercise just gives you a headache and you decide simply to call your company Something, you're too late. The Some Thing Group already exists in Japan (www. sthd.co.jp).

Not only does the marketer need to find something somewhat original and attention grabbing, he also needs a name that will "sound right" when read and spoken. My company is currently looking to brand a service and, in the process, tie together a Web domain name and toll-free phone number. It's been difficult to find options that match all of the criteria: be original, stand out, and don't sound goofy.

I got a laugh from an article that has been passed around the Web. The article lists the most unfortunately named Web site Uniform Resource Locators, or URLs. I investigated, found, and omitted the usual couple of hoaxes that found their way into the article, and, in the process, found additional and legitimately horrible domain names. Here are the highlights (or perhaps lowlights):

If you're looking to find the name of the agent who represents a particular celebrity, then of course you might legitimately search using a phrase such as "who represents." Yet if you use that phrase as the URL for a subscription site, as have the owners of www.whorepresents.com, then you should expect a different kind of visitor.

The Mole Station Native Nursery in New South Wales specializes in the production of hardy native shrubs. The owners have changed the main URL to www.molerivemursery.com, but if you type in the former URL, www.molestationnursery.com, you can still get in. It might be time to just snuff out the old URL, don't you think?

A Web portal where programmers exchange advice and links, www.expertsexchange.com, could have used an expert when the portal was being named. The site was recently modified to www.experts-exchange.com. Wonder why.

However, you can't convince me that the art designers who put together www.speedofart.com didn't have some inkling of what they were doing and don't continue to give themselves the giggles.

Given the recent history of layoffs and losses, perhaps the Ford Owners' Association Web site, www.fordowners.org, makes some sense.

Other egregious examples I found include one Phyllis Staines, a Jacksonville, Florida, Realtor who uses her first initial and last name as the basis for her Web site, and an Australian chain of sushi restaurants called Sushi Train (it just doesn't look good when combined as one word).

According to my quick search, www.whydoisoundsostupid.com is wide open.

You have to wonder: didn't the people who came up with those names ask anyone—anyone—to review them beforehand and check for obvious problems? I think there's also a larger, related issue for marketing: when contemplating new names or campaigns, is there a minimum level of input you should get from others before making a decision, and is there also a point of diminishing returns to advice?

Input is good, but certainly there must be limits. I believe two distinctions are important. First, there's the distinction between getting the input of those affected (directly or indirectly) by the decision versus the opinion of those whose work will go on the same either way. Input from those affected serves the dual purpose of attracting informed comments and encouraging buy-in to the ultimate decision. Second, I find a big distinction between getting honest, personal reactions from people, i.e., what they think and how they react, versus the instances where people play marketing strategist and try to guess how others will think and react.

Whether you're using structured market research such as surveys or focus groups, or just having a hallway conversation, it's far more enlightening to keep the focus on individuals' gut reactions. It's your job as the marketer to sort through responses and try to predict how the marketplace will think and react.

Making Sense of Polls

2006

We are in high political season. That means, of course, lots of people are trying to tell you what you think. It also means that lots of people claim to already know what you and all the rest of the voters think and, thus, what will happen come Election Day.

I am not one of those people. I don't know how the votes will go. However, I do know a lot about surveys and how to interpret them. So let's have a refresher—a way to make you a more informed consumer of the deluge of political polls you'll be seeing. Moreover, beyond the political season, it is always good for a marketer to know how to separate diamonds from cubic zirconia when it comes to surveys.

My suggestion is to raise three basic questions of any poll you are presented:

1) Who was asked? Surveys are a way to ask questions of a relatively small number of people as a way to learn what a much larger number of people think and feel. So, one of the fundamentals in survey research is to make sure you can believe that the answers from that small number (the sample) are an accurate window into the brains of the larger number. Anything other than a representative sample is bound to produce BS (a biased survey).

Perhaps the best way to describe a representative sample is to list some decidedly nonrepresentative ones. For example, never trust the results of a survey from toll-free phone numbers or Web sites. Such surveys run afoul of nonresponse bias, meaning that those who respond to the survey differ significantly in terms of their views and passion than those who do not respond. Even worse, such pseudo-polls are easy prey for ballot stuffing. You want to vote twenty times? Visit the Web site twenty times!

Why would any news organization cut corners with a sample? Many err in favor of tight deadlines and limited budgets. Why would any political candidate present results from a biased sample? Puh-lease.

2) How were they asked? Question wording and order are subtle, yet they can have dramatic effects on survey results. Even reasonably reputable organizations can get caught. For example, in 1996 the Pew Research Center asked whether Bill Clinton or Bob Dole was better described by the phrase "shares my values." In that poll, Clinton had a ten-point advantage (47 percent to 37 percent). However, when CBS asked whether each candidate "shares the moral values most Americans try to live by," Dole received 70 percent agreement while Clinton received 59 percent agreement.

Watch for whether survey respondents are asked to give their personal opinion or their opinion of others' opinions. Recognize, too, that certain words trigger certain responses (such as "war" versus "conflict" versus "military action" versus "peacekeeping mission").

Political parties and candidates are the worst offenders when it comes to how questions are worded. A pseudo-poll on housedemocrats.gov asks visitors whether an investigation into the federal response to Hurricane Katrina should come from "an independent commission of experts" or "Republicans in Congress investigating themselves." Wonder how that one will turn out? On the other side of the fence, a pseudo-poll on the National Republican Congressional Committee site asks what visitors believe would be the first order of business for a Democratic-controlled Congress; options include "raise taxes" and "increase wasteful spending."

3) What's the point? When I have consulted business leaders on marketing research, I generally began by asking them what it is they really want to learn. (Were I so inclined, I could manipulate samples and questions to generate almost any number you would want from a survey.) Similarly, as a consumer of polls, I ask myself what is to be accomplished from that poll. It's clear that the candidates and parties want to generate favorable opinions and coverage with their polls. What is less obvious is the stake that news organizations have in reporting poll results. Remember that easily digested bits of conflict and controversy make news, while level-headed discussions of nonresponse bias and sampling error generate yawns. Imagine the motivation behind the poll and you'll likely have a good head start for assessing the results.

I'm Aware of That

2006

It's early December. Now that you have feasted upon holiday turkeys, hams, and perhaps things you actually slew, it's time to skewer a traditional marketing idea in honor of the new year. I propose we put a fork in the idea of "building awareness" as a marketing goal.

I advanced this notion a few months ago during a presentation to a chapter of the Sales & Marketing Executives Association. That prompted some discussion and debate, as it's counter to what many other marketers have been preaching for years. My thought—then and now—is that really good marketers are ultimately trying to get consumers to do something measurable in the marketplace. We want you to buy our stuff, of course, although there are other business-building behaviors that are good as well: referring friends, actively seeking information, posting messages online for others to see.

Note that it's "behavior" we're talking about here, and the world is full of cases where behavior and awareness seem to be independent of each other. For example, are any American adults not aware by now that smoking is bad for health? And yet I still hear public-health advocates talk about generating awareness among Americans about the risks of smoking.

A traditional model of persuasion holds that consumers pass through a sequence of stages before buying. Most commonly taught is a four-stage process of awareness, interest, preference, and action. I think that model holds true in some instances—but even when it does, awareness is, by definition, only an introductory step.

Several fast-food operators looked at consumer research about the prospects of including healthier menu options in their stores. The research consistently showed that more Americans are aware of the caloric and fat content of their favorite burgers and fries, understand the implications for their personal health, and even have good intentions to select healthier foods. So what happened to all of those healthier selections on fast-food menus? Let's just say that those selections were typically not selected.

Recently I was invited to participate in a daylong "marketing leadership roundtable" in Chicago sponsored by the Corporate Executive Board. During our lunch, I mentioned to a few other CMO types my disdain for the way the Holy Grail of Awareness is touted in certain quarters. That hit a nerve. "Tell me about it!" said one CMO as she nearly jumped out of her chair. "I'm aware that I'm not thirty years old anymore, but that doesn't mean I can do a thing about it. If one more vendor tells me they're going to build awareness for me, I think I'll just scream."

The following day I was speaking to some advertising agency folks about my goals for the brands I lead and likewise mentioned that "awareness is a big yawner for me." The reaction was far different. Faces were blank. The pause was lengthy. Finally, someone asked, "Could you tell me more about that? I would think that generating awareness would be a good thing for you, seeing as how you're rebuilding the Mountain Valley brand."

Happy to explain, I said. It isn't that awareness is a bad thing or even that it may not be, in many cases, a necessary first step toward a behavioral goal (such as a consumer buying something from you). After all, people rarely buy things of which they are unaware. At the same time, however, awareness does not produce those behavioral outcomes—which are ultimately what we as marketers are trying to achieve. Just because you are aware of something doesn't mean you believe it, have an opinion of it, think it's better or worse than anything else—or especially that you're going to trade your money for it. Unless an agency, research firm, consultant, or anyone else can show potential clients that they can move a brand beyond awareness, I advised, they will generate more of the disdain that I see among senior corporate marketers.

Let me know whether you think I'm on the mark or misguided. But I will leave you with one final thought: Do you think most Americans were aware that they might eat and spend too much during the holidays? If so, do you think that mattered?

Debating Awareness

Considering the volume of feedback you offered from my most recent column ("I'm Aware of That"), one might have thought I was advocating the end of college football bowl games.

As it was, I merely passed along the disconnect many marketing decision-makers feel between the results they and their CEOs expect (typically financial ones) and the promised result of "awareness-building" that many consultants, ad agencies, and media salespeople tend to trumpet.

The e-mails I received were all thoughtful. Reactions tended to fall into one of two camps: either "you hit the nail on the head, Brother Jim" (from other marketing directors and some agency types) or "you're underestimating the importance of awareness" (from media and other agency types).

Upon further review, I am sticking to my original assertion that, although awareness is, in some limited instances, a necessary intermediate step toward some measurable marketing goal, it is an inappropriate goal by itself. Here are three points that both address some of your comments and, I hope, clarify that assertion.

1) Can all good things be measured?

A few readers pointed out that marketers will never be able to reliably measure every result from their efforts. Typical was this: "Marketers are dreaming if they think all of their spending and marketing will be quantifiable and trackable."

This isn't an issue confined to mushy marketing stuff. Even hard-nosed physical scientists have their issues with measurement. In August 2006 astronomers officially downgraded the planet Pluto to "dwarf planet" status. Pluto itself didn't change last year, yet expert humans' assessment of Pluto did. Just thought I'd point that out.

In any event, a debate about the role of awareness is not a debate about what is and is not measurable. After all, there are several well-accepted ways of measuring awareness. In fact, the metrics for assessing awareness are years ahead of those used for measuring customer loyalty or word-of-mouth communication. However, those latter two areas are still far more interesting to CMOs than is awareness. Why do you think that is?

2) A means versus an end.

One agency leader took my admission that "people rarely buy things of which they are unaware" and wrote that it was itself "evidence of the importance of awareness as part of a comprehensive marketing strategy."

And who can argue with that? Not I, although awareness should only be a step in your marketing strategy if you are legitimately trying to get your market to understand or do something that is new or unexpected to it. One need look no further than the efforts to promote business relocations or tourist visits to Arkansas; lots of potential customers outside our borders don't have this state on their minds. Putting it there is a necessary and laudable short-term goal.

Still, even in those instances, awareness isn't even close to the end game. As I said in my last column, "Just because you are aware of something doesn't mean you believe it, have an opinion of it, think it's better or worse than anything else—or especially that you're going to trade your money for it." To their great credit, I believe that the folks leading tourism marketing in Arkansas, for example, understand this; they spend time and money measuring intermediate steps such as consumer perceptions as well as desired end results such as room-nights. But some of you still need to pipe down about awareness because...

3) Perception is reality.

I don't claim that my opinion, or the consensus opinion of marketing leaders with whom I have spoken, is representative of all marketers. Nor are we necessarily "right" on this issue. However, anyone who pitches CMO types for a living would be well advised to note the frustration many marketing leaders have for potential suppliers who don't embrace their goals. If enough marketing decision-makers believe that awareness is a useless goal for the dollars they spend, then ad salespeople, agency principals, and other marketing services suppliers need to find—and deliver upon—other ones.

With the average tenure of a big-company CMO now at—yikes—23 months and shrinking, senior marketers won't wait on you to figure all this out.

It's a Fumm-bull!

2007

Back in the day, there was generally one big college football game on the tube any given fall weekend—and the legendary announcer Keith Jackson was in the booth.

Keith is still on your TV, of course, though these days I admit preferring the 1970s-era Keith Jackson on ESPN Classic to the 2007 version. Few sounds were more unusual, more fun to impersonate, or more likely to get you running from the kitchen back to the TV than that of Keith yelling out, "It's a fumm-bulll... and OAK-la-HOME-ahh's got it!"

Recently, as a retail customer, I had an experience that left Keith's voice ringing in my ears. Attempting to get through part of the honey-do list at a big-box store (with two of my boys in tow), I realized that I needed some quick help from another department. That other department was empty, so I did what most red-blooded, demanding, time-limited, and relatively lazy shoppers would do: I asked the nearest uniformed associate how I could get some help.

Now, there might be a better term for this service encounter, but I refer to it as "the handoff." The handoff occurs when one customer-service person needs to move the ball (the shopper or caller) to another customer-service person who can, it is hoped, then provide the needed result.

It's difficult for retailers to achieve consistency with the hand-off. Customer-service workers, being human beings and all, tend to want to focus on their immediate tasks. Plus, I suspect that the number of handoffs rises and falls with overall store or phone traffic; when things are very busy, it might seem impossible to deal with a handoff.

But the handoff is also an opportunity to shine and get the big play. Your customer-service protocol should include training and incentives around the handoff. It's entirely predictable that this will be part of the store or call center experience, so it is wise to plan for success. It's also a high-return activity; by definition you already have the prospective customer within your grasp (either in your store or perhaps on the phone), and you will likely have success as long as you hold onto the ball.

The actual customer-service behavior I have seen has ranged from "that's not my job" (think Freddie Prinze in *Chico and the Man*) to vague promises of someone else showing up later to the customer-service person taking full responsibility—and even personal satisfaction—in making sure the issue is resolved by his associate.

In my case a few days ago, the nearest associate was moving some items around on a shelf but not engaged with another customer. Nevertheless, he didn't make eye contact (uh-oh... you'd better look the ball in), nor did he even direct me to get help (the ball is loose...it's a fumm-bulll!).

What should have happened? Many high-end, service-intensive businesses have strict guidelines for the handoff. At most Marriott hotels, for example, guests asking for directions to a gift shop, meeting room, or the like are to be personally led to their correct destination. That level of service isn't possible in every type of business, of course, though I suspect executives at this big-box retailer would have cringed at my experience. A reasonable expectation might have involved directing me to the specific location where help would be provided, making a call for assistance, and getting a confirmation call back when the handoff was complete.

Whatever the level of service you expect from your associates, it should be specified, reinforced, and rewarded. I know of cases in which, for example, inventory managers were expected to always pitch in to help store shoppers yet chided if they took time from an inventory task in order to do just that.

Here's hoping your business has more good handoffs and fewer "Whoa, Nellie" moments.

What's in Your Baggage?

2007

Ahhh, September...time for the season we've been anticipating since January. There s just the slightest hint of a break from the sweltering summer heat. It's a time when your team is again undefeated, energized, and feeling ready for all challenges. Let the games begin!

You weren't thinking about football, were you? No, it's time for the really big game: planning and budgeting for 2008. (OK, while strategic planning lacks the pageantry and immediate gratification of high school, college, or pro football games, it can involve a similar degree of excitement, fear, and overconsumption.)

Much as a coach should have a very good understanding of his team's weaknesses so that he can plan strategies to get around them, you can recognize your team's inherent weaknesses in making strategic decisions.

The TV ads for a brand of credit cards pose the question, "What's in your wallet?" Let's stipulate that your team—like any team—will bring a lot of baggage (far bigger than a wallet) to the upcoming planning season.

The fact is that every individual brings to the group process some baggage in the form of biases and distortions. None of us is wired or socialized to be a completely cool, objective evaluator of imperfect or conflicting bits of information.

Although everyone is a bit different, there are nevertheless a few common biases that almost any human being carries around to some degree. Compounded across individuals, the impact of these biases on strategic planning and budgeting teams in the arena of business—very social and human processes—is thus enormous. If you can recognize ahead of time the ways such biases can skewer and devour your planning processes and results, then you and your management colleagues stand a very good chance of doing a better job than your competitors.

Two of the most powerful biases in judgment might appear to be opposite ingredients that, when combined in the boiling pot of a large-scale planning process, might cancel each other out. The more common outcome is that these biases work in different ways at different decision points in the typical planning process. Sometimes, they might even combine for a nasty and destructive interaction.

The first big bias to understand is overoptimism. Business leaders, being human and all, tend to overestimate the likelihood of positive outcomes from their decisions. The unseen lever that pushes that bias is overconfidence. We can see this overconfidence in many arenas. For example, a host of surveys reveals that most Americans believe they are in the top fifth of the population in a range of skills from driving to stock-picking. (Even Garrison Keillor's fictional Lake Wobegon is full of children who are "all above average.")

Overoptimism is most pronounced when there is little data or precedent to rein it in. Therefore, if your team is planning into relatively unknown territory, your team should consider the use of case studies, decision trees with specific probabilities assigned, or any other tools that will make everyone consider future challenges with a clearer eye.

The second big piece of cognitive baggage to understand is improper loss aversion, or the assignment of more value to potential losses than to potential gains. This bias mangles strategic decision making by freezing executives into a state of inaction, even when the risks involved in a decision are objectively acceptable.

Perhaps surprisingly, loss aversion doesn't rear its head as often for the really big, expensive, and risky decisions. (In those cases, overoptimism from the company's leadership tends to kick in.) Rather, it's the small to medium stuff such as brand extensions, minor product launches, or smaller acquisition decisions that suffer most.

People often get stuck in loss aversion because they naturally consider each option as an uncomfortable change from a known status quo. A better way to evaluate options—and blunt the impact of loss aversion—is to consider each risky decision not in isolation but as one of many risky decisions to be made over the course of time (a portfolio, if you will).

I would be interested to read your thoughts on these decision biases and how your organization works to keep the baggage light.

More Than a Box

2007

It has been called "the final three feet" and "the final three seconds" of consumer decision making. Packaging, which involves decisions ranging from design to materials and more, has always been an important component of the marketing mix. With the convergence of greater competition, environmental pressures, and consumers' demands for eye-catching aesthetics with hard-nosed functionality, packaging decisions are assuming an even more vital role these days.

Some of the more notable recent innovators I've noticed include Jones Soda (whose packages feature photos submitted by customers), Sherwin-Williams (its "Ready to Roll" combines a paint container and roller tray into a single, recyclable package), and Cargo Cosmetics (which introduced a single-use, highly portable ColorCard eye shadow that's the size of a credit card). So what's happening at the leading edge of the packaging world now? A lot, actually, as I learned just this month.

I had the honor of speaking at the fifth annual Packaging That Sells conference, staged at the Drake Hotel in Chicago by *Brand Packaging* magazine. Other speakers came from heavyweights such as GlaxoSmithKline, Procter & Gamble, Honeywell, and Hewlett-Packard. Numerous design firms, retailers, and suppliers were well represented, too.

Following my talk, once I had the opportunity to listen, I heard some great case studies that are still being written in the marketplace. Here are four imperatives that were woven throughout the success stories I heard:

* Make it smaller. Paul Vracui of Procter & Gamble described how P&G's entire liquid laundry detergent lineup (Tide, Gain, Era, Dreft, and Cheer) is being converted to "2X" concentrated formulas by April 2008; this is part of a broad corporate initiative for reducing the size of and materials in packaging. It's the biggest change in P&G's laundry detergent line in fifteen years.

* Get consumers involved in the process. Kevin McLaughlin of Mike's Hard Lemonade and Brendan Light of Buzzback Market Research described an online research project that the Mike's team used for making final design decisions on their new six-pack case of Mike's Hard Tea. A carefully screened research panel of four hundred consumers dragged, dropped, and voted on a secure Web site from among three color schemes, three font styles, and three versions of a lemon visual. Professional designers created the options, so the ultimate choice would be within brand guidelines. The research design was thus a bit like comparing three sport coats, three shirts, and three ties in a store in order to find the best single combination.

When done correctly, a process of involving customers in your designs not only enhances loyalty among your customers but also minimizes the inevitable internal disagreements between design and production factions within your team. After all, when it's time to decide among several options, who can argue with, "This is what we know our customers want"?

* Clean the clutter. Every logo and/or label redesign discussed at the conference had as its goal a reduced number of visual elements. Time after time, I heard executives complain that their look had become "too busy" over time—which affected the clarity of their messages to consumers. When in doubt, cut it out.

* Fast, fast, fast. Getting package innovations to market quickly was a big topic as well. Many of the bigger consumer-products companies—notorious in the past for taking their own sweet time with even the smallest package changes—are acting more nimbly. Popular methods for getting the lead out of time-to-market include forcing accountability onto cross-functional (research, design, and manufacturing) teams and, as mentioned above, using speedier methods of gathering data and doing research.

Yes, the marketplace winners are doing a lot more out there than just trotting out "New and Improved" or "Bonus Size" all over again. In particular, the emphases on customer involvement and efficient decision making are great lessons for anyone involved in marketing.

Worries at the Summit

2007

Do the marketing leaders of the biggest, most influential players around the world worry about the same things as you and I? I recently had a unique vantage point from which to hear, discuss, and share with you the answers to that very question. You might be surprised—and even reassured—by the result.

Early in November, I had the privilege of serving as honorary chairman of the semiannual Chief Marketing Officer Summit, held this time in Colorado Springs and staged by the Marcus Evans Co.

The format combined a series of sixty- or ninety-minute presentations from CMOs and several "marketer-only" meals and events. The lineup of speakers included marketing leaders from Ford Motor Co., Symantec, AXA Equitable, Vonage, MySpace. com, Pacer International, YRC Worldwide, and Kmart. There were also about ninety nonspeaker attendees.

I couldn't help but notice, as a side note, that among those seven aforementioned speakers, only three individuals were white males. Perhaps the marketing executive suite is changing along with the American consumer marketplace.

In my role as chair, I gave the opening keynote address ("The CMO as Public Relations Leader"). I also introduced the other CMO speakers and was generally able to spend lots of individual quality time with these marketing leaders. We also had less-structured time to get together in smaller groups and talk about anything and everything marketing that was on our minds. (It was, after all, a meeting of marketers; beverages were served.)

As it turns out, the current work and worries of these leaders break out evenly on opposite sides of the spectrum—a combination of highfalutin concepts and strategy plus the gritty realities of getting people in the marketing organization to work together.

First, there is the strategic challenge. Today's marketing leader must make sure the company's marketing strategy puts the company in the right game with the right assets for the right reasons. The strategy must be both tightly focused (customer segments, competitive differentiation, and position) and also flexible enough to enable the company to adapt to rapidly changing market conditions.

But that's the relatively easy part for highly accomplished marketing leaders. These folks understand branding, research, segmentation, defending a niche, anticipating competitors' reactions, and all the other building blocks of a sound marketing strategy. (If they didn't, they likely wouldn't be highly accomplished marketing leaders.)

The harder element comes in coordinating the marketing strategy with an overall corporate strategy—and making sure that marketing activities are measured and tracked against the bigger corporate picture. Part of the fear is doubtless due to

CMOs' precarious positions; an oft-quoted statistic at the conference was a claim from the executive-recruitment firm Spencer Stuart putting CMOs' average job tenure at twenty-three months. Here are four speakers' topics that highlight the point: "Proving the Connection Between Marketing's Capabilities and Corporate Growth," "Cultivating a Strategic Perspective," "Drawing the Link Between Your Marketing Organization and Corporate Strategies," and "Two Shall Become One: Marketing and Corporate Strategy."

Secondly, there is the constant challenge of leading and coordinating one's marketing team. Even at their high organizational levels, the CMOs with whom I spoke all spent a lot of time with teamwork basics—identifying common goals, sharing information, creating common resources, and communicating effectively. For example, Lisa Bacus, the head of global marketing strategy for Ford, spoke on "Nurturing Your Marketing Organization."

I wondered aloud during lunch one day why, with so much research and discussion out there about organizational effectiveness, we still have to work so hard in order to break down silos in our companies. "I guess," came the reply from a CMO, "it's because companies are populated with human beings!"

So, whether your marketing budget ends with a few zeros or many (and whether your support staff is extensive or can be fully seen in your mirror), find comfort in the fact that marketers at all levels are pursuing similar ends and dealing with similar issues. How are you addressing them in your company?

Is Your CEO a Marketer?

2008

What are today's most powerful corporate leaders like—and how did they get to the top? The noted executive-search firm Spencer Stuart conducts an annual survey to answer just those sorts of questions, and the latest numbers are out. I believe they carry some important implications for marketing effectiveness.

Some of the notable characteristics of CEOs of the Standard & Poor's 500 companies include:

* CEOs are getting younger. Since 1980, the average age of top-company CEOs has decreased from fifty-nine to fifty-six (even while people are living and working longer overall).

* Today's CEO is increasingly likely to have had international experience.

* CEOs get graduate degrees. Two-thirds of all S&P 500 CEOs have earned some type of advanced degree, with the MBA by far the most popular (held by 40 percent of all CEOs). Among non-MBA advanced degrees, a law degree and a Ph.D. rank as most frequent.

* CEOs are coming to their jobs with a greater variety of functional experiences. In 2000, about one-quarter of top CEOs

had been in one functional area throughout their careers; today, that number is a measly 9 percent.

I find the results on functional paths to the CEO position particularly interesting. You should, too, if you want to climb to the top of the ladder. After all, you have a large degree of control over that variable.

From the 2007 Spencer Stuart data, we learn that operations (at 24 percent) was the most popular functional role held by an individual before becoming CEO. Finance (22 percent) and marketing (14 percent) roles were next. Only 8 percent of big-company CEOs had followed a purely general management functional path throughout their careers, down from 12 percent in both 2006 and 2005.

Although these surveys provide an interesting snapshot of America's corporate leadership—including CEOs' most commonly traveled paths to the top—they don't address effective CEO performance ("being the CEO" as opposed to just "becoming the CEO").

There is a consensus among executive recruiters, investors, and board-level consultants that a CEO's attention to marketing and sales explains much of that CEO's chances for success at the helm. It is a hypercompetitive marketplace with fewer barriers to entry in most industries, a shortening half-life for new products and ideas, and greater control in the hands of consumers. If you don't understand the consumer and how to meet the quickly evolving needs of the marketplace, then it is difficult to imagine how you can generate returns for shareholders.

My view—likely biased—is that it is more difficult for marketing professionals to gain a CEO post because they often lack true P&L accountability. Operations executives can show facility in running the business efficiently, while financial hotshots and lawyers are skilled in connecting with investors and making deals to build the company. But who is best suited to grow the company once in charge?

If you're the aspiring-CEO type, then it makes sense to get a mix of experiences across disciplines. Put marketing at or near the top of your list of experiences and education, because you will need a sophisticated understanding of the marketing discipline to excel once you earn that corner office. For example, while only one in seven CEOs (14 percent) came to the role immediately following a marketing post, another 13 percent have worked in a marketing position at some point in their careers.

If you're one of those CEOs without marketing expertise, then resolve to take some simple yet profound steps that will both educate you and signal to your colleagues that you have the appropriate customer focus.

* Allocate much if not most of your visible time to customers, prospects and customer-facing employees.

* Champion the marketing function and marketing colleagues inside the company. If you know people better than you know marketing, then get great marketing people and keep them focused and motivated

* Groom the next generation of company leaders with meaningful marketing training and experience.

Note: All of this advice comes from an undergraduate finance major.

Recession Resistance

2008

Although the National Bureau of Economic Research ultimately decides whether we're in an official recession, those of us in business tend to believe a period of negative real economic growth has already begun. As with stormy weather, we can look to forecasts and guess as to the downturn's length and severity, but in the meantime, businesses simply have to deal with it. So how should you adjust your marketing efforts in a recession? Is it slash-and-burn time? Or is there a case to be made for staying in the game (even when it hurts)?

Marketing expenditures tend to be one of the first corporate casualties during lean times. Several executives I know tell me that while the rational sides of their brains are lobbying for continued investment in marketing, the pressure to cut any discretionary dollars can be overwhelming.

However, the numbers tell us that if you can possibly weather the storm, recessions are actually a high-return investment opportunity.

Remember the early 1980s? The recession of 1981–82 was a doozy: The national unemployment rate peaked at 10.8 percent, and the prime lending rate reached 21.5 percent. It was an awful time for business investment, yet those corporate leaders who set their jaws and stayed the course were eventually rewarded handsomely (as were the shareholders).

How handsomely? McGraw-Hill Research studied the marketing spending of six hundred U.S. companies during 1980–85. After the 1987 numbers were available, McGraw-Hill concluded that the companies that maintained or increased their advertising during the 1981–82 recession showed an average sales gain of 275 percent during the subsequent five-year period. Those companies that cut advertising during 1981–82 grew sales by an average of only 19 percent during the same period.

In 2002—with the slowdown of 2000–01 fresh in executives' minds—researchers Gary Lilien and Arvind Rangaswamy of Penn State's Smeal College of Business interviewed more than 150 senior marketers from a variety of industries. Their respondents said that companies meeting three criteria could gain market share during a recession. Firms that already have a strategic emphasis on marketing, an entrepreneurial culture, and a sufficient reserve of capital come out winners.

None of this is to suggest that you shouldn't be especially active in managing marketing efforts when the storm is raging. Efficiency and focus become even more important. Here are some moves you might consider:

* Adjust the product mix. Buyers still need to buy, yet the emphasis moves more strongly to functional benefits during a recession.

* Shore up the distribution channel. Channel partners need your help, and this is a great opportunity to gain competitive advantage with superior ideas and service. A recession also

clearly illustrates where you have weak distributors; use the opportunity to cull the herd so that you're best positioned for the inevitable recovery and expansion.

* Avoid the temptation to go cheap. If you lessen the value of your offerings or bolt to lower-priced channels, then your brands unfortunately will lose long-term value.

* Stay close to customers. Consider the opportunities to up-sell and cross-sell current customers before cutting prices (and benefits) to chase new ones.

* Stay visible. As the evidence presented above shows, a consistent level of advertising and public relations will mean relative advantage over those competitors who indiscriminately cut marketing funds and go into hiding.

Americans are a-Changin'

2008

Are you a skeptic when it comes to books, programs, and media reports about the latest "this will change the world forever" trend? I am, and I believe that is a healthy trait for business executives. When I hear someone say "if current trends continue," I tend to drastically discount the value of the subsequent prediction. (I still remember the 1980-ish column in my hometown's weekly newspaper breathlessly declaring that "the leisure suit is here to stay.")

It's more common that things run cyclically rather than in endless growth streams. Projected trends in the economy, design, migration, or natural resources—even from the experts—often don't play out. However, one set of widely publicized projections is actually happening more quickly than was originally anticipated.

In 2004, the U.S. Census Bureau had estimated that non-Hispanic whites would cease to be the racial majority in America by the year 2050. Now the government has released new projections that actually move that landmark point ahead by eight years, to 2042. The increasing rates of immigration and births among minorities have fueled this increased pace of diversity.

Long before 2042, however, the changing face of America will have led to profound changes in the winners and losers in American business.

Here are some of the highlights from the Census Bureau's updated projections:

* By 2017, the Social Security system will have reached the point when payouts exceed collections. Consider the sense of urgency and opportunity this will mean to financial institutions.

* By 2023, minorities will comprise more than half of all American children under the age of five. Toy manufacturers, day-care providers, and educational leaders should be paying close attention to the implications.

* By 2030, those age sixty-five or older will make up one-fifth of the American population. What will that mean for travel, investing, and health care?

* By 2042, whites will cease to be a majority of the population.

* By 2050, Hispanics will account for 30 percent of the population (rising from 15 percent today), while Asians will account for more than 9 percent of the total (compared with 5 percent today).

* The total U.S. population will have grown from the current 305 million people to 439 million.

Other imperatives for marketing plans abound in these numbers. The growth of Hispanic households—with their larger average sizes—plus the changing composition of other American households of the future are big news to architects, contractors, and real estate agents as they plan, buy, and sell houses, apartments, and assisted-living facilities. Manufacturers of products such as greeting cards, playground equipment, maternity wear, theater seating, and pet items must understand the dynamics of family relationships, household location, and personal mobility. Media and technology companies need to innovate with relevant content and new ways to distribute it.

At the same time, traditional consumer-goods companies must continue to make good decisions about ingredients, product design, and labeling. How must educational institutions adapt in terms of curricula, funding, and the overall distribution of learning opportunities? What are the implications for recruiting and training the future members of your marketing team?

Before we get too carried away, of course, it's worth noting that census numbers are aggregates; you can't depend on them for precise insights as to your customers or best prospects. Nevertheless, smart marketers can blend what they already know about their customers and organizations with this updated population data to create powerful segmentation strategies.

If you haven't yet embraced the concept of disciplined market segmentation and put it to work for your business, well, you're a laggard. You do have time to adjust and take advantage of the changes and inevitable opportunities that profoundly changed demographics will produce. But the landscape is already changing, and the pace is picking up.

Why Snuggie Sells

2009

In an economy where seemingly no one is buying anything, you might feel downright cozy after reading this statistic: According to *Advertising Age,* the makers of the Snuggle blanket have sold more than four million units in less than four months.

That's right. The blanket with sleeves, that star of direct-response ads all over cable TV, the recipient of my vote as the second cheesiest national ad on the air right now—trailing only the Loud 'N' Clear "personal sound amplifier" earpiece—is selling so quickly that Allstar Marketing Group of Hawthorne, New York, is carrying nearly zero inventory. The waiting period for delivery is four to six weeks from the time of your phone call.

Wouldn't you like your business to be in busy-order-taker mode right now?

Direct-response TV experts have told me that most companies simply strive to break even on their advertising campaigns (sales margin from the product, less media time and production costs) until they can secure full distribution at retail. According to Allstar Marketing Group, the Snuggle is projected to be profitable during 2009 even before the distributors gain a retail foothold. The company first got its product onto shelves at

Walgreen's and Bed Bath & Beyond and hopes to be in Wal-Mart before the year is over.

Without a doubt, the success of the Snuggle is partially due to fortunate timing. More importantly, however, those numbers are a product of someone being smart enough to put the product in a position to win.

* Position your product for the times. The Snuggle is a great fit for the cut-back-and-be-practical environment of today. As consumers are spending more time at home and looking for ways to cut costs, the appeal of a no-frills product is still strong. In addition, there is the usual set of free stuff so common in direct-response ad: a BOGO (Buy One Get One) free offer plus a clip-on book light. Almost any consumer can feel comfortable with this expenditure.

* Media advertising is a big bargain if you have the product and message. Many traditional media outlets—daily newspapers, broadcast TV—are hurting. You can find a great deal of media time and space available these days at very attractive pricing. If you have a product and message ready, then there is great opportunity to keep costs low, negotiate added bang for your bucks, and pave the way for a compelling return on investment.

* Keep it real. There's little in the way of *haute couture* when it comes to the Snuggie (unless the "huggable monk" look is big on the fashion runways). This product is all about practicality. The company isn't trying to make the product something it isn't. In fact, the somewhat goofy look of the Snuggie has propelled viral marketing successes, such as a customer-created

Facebook page with more than ten thousand fans the last time I checked.

* Lead with a problem-solving message. Capitalizing on the Snuggie's fit for the times, the brand messaging has avoided any mention of imagery and instead has focused squarely on solving consumer problems. An e-mail ad I received for the Snuggle used this headline: "Lower Your Heating Bills!"

* Get out there (at low risk). Perhaps the biggest lesson here is that consumers are still buying (some) stuff and companies are making money. The direct-response approach—such as TV ads and e-mails created to get an order right now from the end customer—is a good one for keeping most costs variable and testing different approaches. Every decent direct marketer I know uses split-half and/or other testing approaches in the field with real consumers, which makes tracking responses and making adjustments a snap.

Now might be just the time for your business to bring innovative ideas to market as well.

Making Social Media Work

2009

This column is neither a breathless ode to social media nor an overly skeptical "have you noticed the dropout rate on Twitter?" rant. My recent speaking and consulting engagements tell me that it's simply time for a reality check and guide to social media—from a business decision-maker's perspective. (Note from the title that I am putting "work" in the same breath as "social.")

For guidance I enlisted Mack Collier, a friend who also happens to be one of the nation's top bloggers (his blog the Viral Garden consistently ranks in the top fifteen, according to FeedBurner) and an insightful consultant to many companies for their social-media efforts (I recommend visiting MackCollier.com). I asked Mack several provocative questions about blogs, social-media tools, and their relevance for people doing business.

Q: Are there specific keys to making a blog successful for business?

A: The biggest mistake most businesses make when they launch a blog is thinking how they can use it to promote themselves. They should think instead about who they want to be reading the blog, and what value it creates for those readers.

This is a big shift in mind-set for many companies, because they want to view social media as a new promotional channel.

It isn't. Social media, no matter what form you use, is simply a communication tool.

As for what you should blog about—you can still leverage your blog as a tool to ultimately promote your business, but do it indirectly. If your company sells cameras, then blog about photography and how to take better pictures. If you sell pet supplies, share "Ten Steps to Giving the Perfect Dog Bath."

Q: How do you rate sites such as Facebook, MySpace, and Twitter in terms of their potential for business?

A: It's not about the tools, but rather the people who will be using the tools.

It doesn't make sense to use the hot new hammer that everyone is buzzing about if the job requires a drill. In order to determine what (if any) social media tools your business should be using, I would ask these questions:

* How many people, and how much time, can be devoted to your social media efforts? Social media requires a ton of time. And like anything else, the more time you can commit, the better your results, on average. I am constantly contacted by companies that want to launch a new blog, that want to be on Facebook and on Twitter.

When I ask how many people will handle all this, they say, "Well, *I* will." That's probably not enough.

* Why do you want to use a blog/Facebook/Twitter? Do some research to figure out where those people you want to reach are today and which tools they are using. It makes no sense to launch a Twitter presence if all your current and potential customers are on LinkedIn. I think every company should have a social media monitoring system in place; use free tools such as Google Blog Search and Twitter Search to see what people are saying about you, your company, your competitors, and your industry.

Q: How do you counsel businesses in tying social-media tools to their Web sites and even their offline marketing efforts?

A: Ultimately you want to use social media tools to create value for others, and that value creation raises your awareness with current and potential customers. But you need to capitalize on that raised awareness by giving customers the ability to get in touch with you, to learn more about you, and maybe even buy. In other words, you want to move them to the next level and use that added interest to your advantage.

One example we are seeing is businesses giving away codes on Twitter that customers can then use for offline sales. This is also a good way to track the effectiveness of Twitter (and you could do this on your blog as well).

This leads to perhaps the most important tip: When you launch social media efforts, make sure you have some way to measure your efforts and track effectiveness in ways that are relevant to business.

Will Your New Products Win?

2009

Even with all of the necessary hatch-battening lately in the business world, most companies still need a regular stream of successful new product or service offerings to prosper over the long haul. Perhaps your company is one that needs to get some new stuff on the market, and soon.

Yet most companies' product introductions aren't survivors. In mature product categories such as automotive supply, new-product success rates (defined as marketplace survival for five years or more) run between 30 percent and 50 percent. In consumer products more generally, the survival rate is typically estimated at 15 percent to 20 percent. For technology products, success might come to fewer than one in ten new entrants.

That isn't a batting average that will keep you in the big leagues very long. But a few companies tend to consistently produce winners. What can you learn from them?

Procter & Gamble is one of those consistent winners. The company's former CEO, A. G. Lafley, said in an April interview with *Business Week* that his company built a 50 percent success rate with new products, which makes P&G roughly three times as successful with new products as the average consumer goods producer. Lafley, who stepped down last month, moved

P&G from a product-oriented model of innovation to one that put the consumer at the center.

A similar culture exists at S. C. Johnson & Son, makers of brands such as Ziploc and Drano. The company has a big hit this summer with its Off clip-on fan, designed mostly for women who would rather not apply chemicals to their skin. Johnson has revitalized its product-development efforts in part by involving marketing managers earlier in the process.

"But Jim," you might say, "my business isn't a consumer-products behemoth. How does this help me?" Fair enough. Here are some market-tested ways to raise your batting average with new products and services, regardless of company size or industry category.

* Seek home runs in the form of clear product advantages. The Off fan is a different type of product for S. C. Johnson. I can imagine how, in other companies, that particular product idea would have been shot down by those who were invested in the notion that repellents simply must be applied to skin. Think differently about consumer needs and don't be afraid to buck the system.

* Do the homework first. In a report for the Product Development Institute, Robert Cooper found that U.S. companies on average devoted only 7 percent of a project's funding to critical up-front activities such as market and competitive analyses, consumer research, concept testing, and technical/feasibility assessments. That can't be sufficient for establishing a real business case. On the other hand, companies that do a better job of predevelopment work have more success and stronger financial returns.

* Integrate the consumer, and your marketing team, into every major point of the process. Consider using workshops, interviews, or focus groups at early, hypothesis-generating stages—then larger-scale, more scientific techniques to validate the most promising ideas.

* Build cross-functional teams, guided by objective financial criteria and a strong project leader accountable for the entire process.

* Define the product with discipline. Development teams should be able to write in ten or fewer pages a coherent case that includes the new product's value for the consumer; its fit with larger strategic objectives and the portfolio; its pricing, distribution, and communication plans; and a justification for financial investment.

* Plan for the launch well in advance. Some teams treat the launch as something to worry about later (in the unlikely event of project approval!).

A reminder to the CEO: Your role is to ensure the discipline and vitality of the entire product-development process—and not to be involved in individual projects. By encouraging both innovation and accountability, you will help develop a solid batting average for all.

Avoiding Failure

2009

Why do failing businesses fail in the first place? Is it typically bad luck, unfortunate timing, lack of capital, an inferior product or service, incompetent management, or some sour combination of all of those factors? Could better marketing make a difference?

I recently had the opportunity to meet and work with Bill Rancic, a successful entrepreneur several times over. You might know Bill as the first-season winner of Donald Trump's *The Apprentice* show on NBC. He founded Cigars Around the World in a four-hundred-square-foot studio apartment years before entering The Donald's universe. Among other ventures, he is now national spokesman for a financial-makeover initiative, Gradient Gives Back. As part of this program, a very deserving Little Rock family was announced as the second national winner and will work with local financial adviser Gary Garrison to get back on their feet.

Bill also hosts *We Mean Business*, a weekly show on the A&E cable network, in which he and a small cadre of experts essentially take over struggling small businesses for a few days and attempt to keep them from failing. I asked Bill his view about the telltale signs of failing businesses—given what he has learned from the thousands of struggling entrepreneurs his team screens for the show—and any advice he could offer.

Bill told me there are three characteristics that tend to describe these failing businesses. First, he said, these businesses are reactive rather than proactive. They can't seem to get ahead of problems and instead spend substantial time and energy putting out fires. Sometimes the business leaders seem to feed off the adrenaline that accompanies crises—but you and I know that's no way to run a business over the long haul.

The second characteristic of failing businesses is that the leaders fail to set goals. It isn't that the entrepreneurs aren't working hard—many of them put in sixty, seventy, or even more hours every week trying to get ahead—but there is often no sense of direction. Over time, everyone becomes frustrated, because there is little sense of accomplishment despite all of the effort that is going into the business.

The third characteristic is that the entrepreneurs aren't thinking big enough. They might have a good product idea but aren't thinking about ways to scale the idea or solve additional customer needs over time. These businesses won't ever be big successes because the owners are failing to create the environment for home runs.

Not surprisingly, I believe that marketing research and sound marketing planning can substantially help to cure each of these three ills. An objective view of the marketplace can help you and your team become more proactive, for example, because you can see weaknesses in your offerings (the way consumers do) and anticipate competitors' moves.

Goal setting is at the heart of a good marketing plan. So are the tactics, resources, and accountabilities that support those goals. If your business doesn't have a detailed marketing plan in place—one that supports and enables the overall business plan—then you might be setting yourself up for Bad Characteristic No. 2. With a marketing plan, however, everyone will understand the big objectives as well as the intermediate goals that let you know you are on the right track.

Good marketing research can also help you avoid the thinking-small trap. By truly understanding your customers, and the benefits they perceive to follow from doing business with you, a business can be agile and exploit big opportunities in the marketplace. Without that understanding, a business is likely to get stuck doing the same things in the same ways.

So, business leader, don't fall into the false belief that research and planning somehow dampen the entrepreneurial spirit. Instead, learn from the problems of other businesses. You can marry your energy and propensity to act with good information and a clear plan. Then maybe your business will be on national TV someday—for the right reasons.

Stop Selling Stuff

2010

Nothing happens, as they say, until someone sells something. Unfortunately, many executives and salespeople are in the habit of saying the wrong things—and thus they miss opportunities to make things happen.

I base this conclusion both on years of published research (among salespeople and buyers) as well as my experiences during the past twelve months working with professional sales teams. The odds are that some of your colleagues involved in sales— outbound, inbound, or frankly any of those with customer-facing roles—are in the rut of pitching stuff, yapping in jargon, or focusing more on their activity levels than on speaking to customer needs.

As part of my affiliation with DSG Consulting, I have been helping client sales teams in industries as diverse as medical technologies, financial services and software, cybersecurity, and Web analytics. Despite the differing dynamics across those industries, the keys to building more effective sales conversations have been remarkably similar.

I am talking business-to-business sales here, by the way, characterized by high price tags and margins, long and complex sales cycles, and other factors that necessitate the care and feeding of professional sales teams. However, the lessons learned are applicable in many B2C (business-to-consumer) settings as well.

In order to secure an appropriate deal in these environments, the sales team has to ultimately get buy-in from a true decision maker at a prospect company. The deal will likely go through accounting or procurement someday (and we love those people), but first it must survive the corporate minefield of tight budgets and competing priorities. It wouldn't surprise you to hear that there is less money sitting around for six- and seven-figure expenditures these days, would it?

The less-successful salespeople tend to live in the world of technical specifications, product demonstrations, reaction to RFPs (requests for proposals), and zillion-slide presentation decks. They are plenty motivated to succeed and they typically know their stuff, mind you, but they often don't fully understand their prospects' businesses or appreciate the results prospects want. Coupled with the pressures of filling out call sheets and trying to hit quotas, these salespeople are performing lots of activities yet are frustrated with the results.

(Pet peeve: Salespeople who substitute questions such as "So what keeps you up at night?" or "Where are you feeling pain these days?" for doing their homework. Were I the prospect, my answers might be "One wife, two dogs, and three kids" and "At this moment, the rear.")

The more successful salespeople follow a different path. They tend to engage in what may be variously called "solution selling," meaning they focus on benefits to the buyer rather than attributes of the product, and "consultative selling," meaning they seek to bring ideas and listening skills to a genuine conversation, rather than wow the prospect with a shiny new object.

This all makes perfect sense—anybody who's anybody in marketing knows to sell benefits rather than features—yet that type of sales behavior is not the norm. The weight of research into salesperson behavior and performance also shows that consultative selling is the way to go.

But it's hard. The path requires research into the prospect's world, a laserlike focus on the prospect's needs (stated and unstated), a certain level of patience, and the resolve to avoid being sucked into a price-driven slap fight with competitors.

Most sales managers aren't helping. According to many self-report surveys, managers admit to spending more time focusing on building volume rather than profitability. They also report having little time or expertise for building the consultative skills of their sales teams.

Executives, you can help by learning how your teams are attempting to engage in solution-driven conversations. I have learned—a bit to my surprise—that even experienced salespeople often lack the confidence necessary to be trusted advisers to customers. Training, practice, and reinforcement within the sales team can produce remarkable results in a few months.

In a time when true product differentiation is rare—and, where it exists, typically short-lived—the way your salespeople act and speak can actually be a competitive advantage. And that can really remove an executive's pain point.

Get Off My Back

2010

It's me, The Consumer. I am back and I have some things to say.

It has been seven years since the last time Dr. Karrh agreed to step aside and let me write one of these columns in his stead. Back then ("Don't Blame Me"), I became annoyed when a Little Rock retailer closed its doors and then in a press release blamed area consumers for "not supporting their entire facility." I felt like I had to remind a few businesspeople about who is responsible to whom in this whole marketing thing. My message then was simple: it isn't my responsibility to support your business if you aren't listening to me and serving my needs.

The seven years that have passed seem like a generation, don't they? Since 2003, I have dealt with war, substantial political and governmental changes, and the deepest economic recession in seventy years. I have to admit that all of this has taken a toll on me.

When it comes to those who are supposed to be looking out for my interests, my opinion has shifted from near ambivalence to basic distrust. In 2004, according to CBS surveys, 47 percent of Americans trusted the federal government to do the right thing most or all of the time. By the fall of 2009, according to the same poll, trust in government had dropped by half—to 23 percent. I don't believe lawmakers or bureaucrats have my back.

My hopes for the future have taken a hit, too. Seven out of ten Americans say it's harder to accumulate wealth today than in the past. That compares to 1999, when only 38 percent of Americans said the same thing (surveys conducted by Princeton Survey Research Associates on behalf of Bankrate.com). At the same time that building wealth is more difficult, the government is planning to take a much bigger chunk for itself. When in recent history has it appeared more difficult to build a legacy?

I would snicker at government attempts to micromanage my behavior if those attempts didn't wind up costing me. As an example, recall the Cash for Clunkers program. Nearly 690,000 vehicles were sold during the time the program was in place. Sounds like Washington flipped a switch and made magic happen, right?

Analysts at Edmunds.com compared historical sales trends and figured out the real story: about 565,000 of those sales would have happened even without the program. The Edmunds study divided the $3 billion program cost by its estimate of 125,000 incremental vehicle sales and concluded that taxpayers shelled out $24,000 for each vehicle actually sold because of the program.

I don't need a convoluted program to begin spending again; I just want an environment where I can spend and save with confidence. Considering that consumer spending drives about two-thirds of the U.S. economy, our state and national leaders should feel a strong interest in creating that environment.

But if you want me back on my feet, then you will first need to get off my back.

I have a history of demonstrating optimism and resilience. I've come back strong after other wars, market crashes, and recessions.

Still, things feel different today. I have had to fundamentally adjust my spending priorities. I worry about deficits, the value of my home, higher taxes, looming inflation, aging parents, and the availability of health care down the road. I am facing the real possibility that the next generation of Consumers will have fewer opportunities than I have had.

So please listen, all of you policymakers and pundits. Serve my needs and I can serve yours. If you will simplify the system, allow me to plan for the long (or even the medium) term, and perhaps let me keep most of my earnings, then I might be able to spend, invest, and pull that economic load as I have in the past.

Just remember that the Consumer, as an average American, is also getting older. My back ain't what it used to be.

www.ingramcontent.com/pod-product-compliance
Lightning Source LLC
Chambersburg PA
CBHW072039190526
45165CB00018B/1154